What Do You Think?

Should Substance-Using Athletes Be Banned for Life?

Neil Morris

Heinemann Library
Chicago, Illinois

Customer Service 888-454-2279
Visit our website at www.heinemannraintree.com

Editorial: Andrew Farrow and Rebecca Vickers
Design: Philippa Jenkins
Picture research: Melissa Allison and Ruth Blair
Production: Alison Parsons

Printed and bound in China

13 12 11 10 09
10 9 8 7 6 5 4 3 2 1

Library of Congress Cataloging-in-Publication Data
Morris, Neil, 1946-
  Should substance-abusing athletes be banned for life? / Neil Morris.
    p. cm. -- (What do you think?)
  Includes bibliographical references and index.
  ISBN 978-1-4329-1676-3 (hc)
  1. Doping in sports--Juvenile literature.
  2. Athletes--Professional ethics--Juvenile literature.
  I. Title.
  RC1230.M68 2008
  362.29--dc22
                            2008014753

Acknowledgments
The publishers would like to thank the following for permission to reproduce photographs:
© Corbis pp. /Ann Johansson 15, /Randy Faris 46, /Tim O'Hara 7, /Tom Grill 4; © Getty Images pp. /AFP 8, 18, 35, 36, /Bongarts 30, /Digital Vision 26, /News 45, /Sport 21, 31, 34; © Masterfile p. 51; © PA Photos pp. 12, 13, 22, 25, 32, 40, /DPA 11; © Photoshot pp. 16, /Talking Sport 43, /UPPA 38; © Kate Shuster p. 48.

Cover photograph: reproduced with permission of © TIPS Images/Bruno Bade/Vandystadt.

Every effort has been made to contact copyright holders of any material reproduced in this book. Any omissions will be rectified in subsequent printing if notice is given to the publishers.

The publishers would like to thank Dr. Robert Weatherby for his assistance with the preparation of this book.

Disclaimer
All the Internet addresses (URLs) given in this book were valid at the time of going to press. However, due to the dynamic nature of the Internet, some addresses may have changed, or sites may have changed or ceased to exist since publication. While the author and publishers regret any inconvenience this may cause readers, no responsibility for any such changes can be accepted by either the author or the publishers.

Table Of Contents

Some words are printed in bold, **like this**. You can find out what they mean in the glossary on pages 54–55.

> *Talk about it*

Sharing your ideas and opinions with your friends will help you to decide what you think about an issue.

What Do You Think?

The aim of this book is to encourage you to form your own opinion about the main question posed by its title: Should substance-using athletes be banned for life? You probably already have your own ideas, but some of the information and quotations from books and articles provided here might persuade you to change your mind. They might at least make you question your own beliefs.

Most people have opinions about important issues. But rather than just having an opinion, it is much better to have an *informed* opinion about an issue. To be informed, you need to approach a subject with an open mind. You can consider the evidence for and against your opinion and then figure out what you think is the best position on the issue. There are lots of different aspects to take into consideration. For example, your overall answer to the big question— Should substance-using athletes be banned for life?— may well be "yes." But you might feel strongly about certain issues, such as treatment of first offenders or the use of certain kinds of drugs and medicines. This book presents many cases and lots of evidence, but it cannot be comprehensive. There are other things you can consider, including the opinions and experiences of your friends and family, as well as information gained from reading other books, magazines, and newspapers.

Critical thinking

As you read this book and think about the issues raised, try to approach the topic using the tools of critical thinking. When we think critically, we set aside our own pre-formed views and ask questions about the information and ideas that are presented to us. This allows us to approach other people's ideas with an open and inquisitive mind. We might ask questions such as these:

- Is this information **biased**? That is, does the writer or speaker have a reason or incentive to present the information in a certain way? Does the opinion based on the information favor one side unfairly without proper reasons being given?
- Is the information *credible* (believable)? Is the point of view supported by good reasons and evidence? Does the evidence presented seem to be reliable?
- What *assumptions* does the writer make? Are facts taken for granted rather than being investigated? Are the assumptions justified or not?
- Do the arguments rely on *sound logic*? Does the writer use good, sensible reasoning in his or her arguments and deductions?
- Does the writer state where the information comes from? If so, does it come from a reliable source?

There are many other questions you might ask of a particular statement. The point of critical thinking is to read texts with an open mind and a skeptical eye, aiming to form your own opinions after paying attention to other people's opinions and ideas.

Informed opinions

You probably already have opinions about the issue of drug abuse in sports. Your views on this subject may be influenced by your opinions on drug abuse in general. But you may not have thought about what the penalties for failing drug tests should be, and you may not know what the current regulations are. In this book you will find the facts, as well as other people's views on those facts. Perhaps you think drug abuse in sports is not such a big deal, but you might think differently after you have read some of the case studies. When you form opinions about these different issues, try to make sure that you express them as arguments. An argument has three parts (A—R—E):

- *Assertion*: An assertion is a strong statement about your opinion.
- *Reasoning*: You should support your assertion with logical reasons.
- *Evidence*: Evidence supports your reasoning by providing facts or examples to show that your argument is valid.

> *Support your viewpoint*

School and public libraries offer a wide range of factual sources for research. You can also look for evidence on the Internet or discuss findings with friends.

✔ Checklist for critical thinking

Critical thinkers . . .

✔ understand the difference between fact and opinion, and are able to distinguish facts from opinions in spoken and written language.

✔ assess the available evidence, evaluating it fairly and completely.

✔ acknowledge different perspectives on an issue, accepting that people may disagree about it, and identify the points of disagreement.

✔ identify assumptions and evaluate them for their validity and any bias.

✔ evaluate different points of view to inform their own opinion.

✔ support their own ideas with sound reasoning and evidence, taking into account conflicting ideas and facts.

> *Gold medalist banned*

U.S. sprinter Justin Gatlin (right) is shown here winning a 200-meter heat at the Athens Olympics in 2004. Gatlin went on to win a gold medal in the 100 meters, silver in the 4 x 100 relay, and bronze in the 200 meters. Two years later, he failed a drug test and received a four-year ban. He had been banned once before, but appealed successfully against it.

What Is Doping?

When an athlete is accused of doping, it means that he or she is thought to have taken drugs ("dope") to improve performance. The term "dope" comes from an old Dutch word meaning "sauce" or "thick liquid," which people must have thought described how drugs looked. So, what are drugs? They can be defined as chemical substances that are introduced into the body to affect the way it functions.

In everyday life, many drugs are legal and can be bought over the counter at a pharmacy or even in a supermarket. People take aspirin tablets and other drugs to help with headaches, and there is a whole range of medicines to fight the effects of colds and flu. Many stronger drugs have to be prescribed by a doctor. Then there are illegal drugs—such as cocaine, heroin, Ecstasy, and marijuana—that are banned in everyday use, as well as in sports.

The drugs that are banned in sports are called "prohibited substances" (see page 13). They include many over-the-counter medicines and **prescription drugs**, as well as illegal substances. Athletes who are caught taking any prohibited substance are usually determined to be cheating, so all athletes have to be very careful about the chemicals and medicines that they use.

Playing fair

You might wonder why we should care whether athletes take drugs or not. The reason is that doping is usually used to improve performance. The world of sports is a competitive business, and if drug-taking were allowed, some athletes would take anything that made them faster or stronger. This would give them an unfair advantage over competitors who did not take drugs.

That is why sports governing bodies condemn doping and label the drug-takers cheaters. Drug-using athletes are going against the spirit of sports and the idea of fair play. According to the rules of sportsmanship, there should always be a "level playing field." This means that all competitors should have the same opportunity to succeed.

✔ The spirit of sports

How would you define the spirit of sports? Here is one definition and a list of values. The motto of the U.S. Anti-Doping Agency is "My health. My sport. My victory. I compete clean." Their definition is as follows:

"Anti-doping programs seek to preserve what is intrinsically valuable about sport. This intrinsic value is often referred to as 'the spirit of sport'; it is the essence of Olympism [the ideals of the Olympic movement]; it is how we play true. The spirit of sport is the celebration of the human spirit, body, and mind and is characterized by the following values:

✔ Ethics, fair play, and honesty
✔ Health
✔ Excellence in performance
✔ Character and education
✔ Fun and joy
✔ Teamwork
✔ Dedication and commitment
✔ Respect for rules and laws
✔ Respect for self and other participants
✔ Courage
✔ Community and solidarity

Doping is fundamentally contrary to the spirit of sport."

[Source: USADA 2007 Guide to Prohibited Substances, www.usantidoping.org]

> *Dangerous drugs*

Birgit Boese was a shot-putter in East Germany (GDR) in the 1980s. From the age of 11, she was given **anabolic steroids** by her coaches to improve her performance. She was told they were vitamins. Today, at age 46, she has severe health problems. She can hardly walk, she has back pain, her liver and kidneys do not function properly, and she has diabetes and asthma.

Health issues

In addition to the question of fair play, there is that of health. Obviously the issue of health problems applies to all drug-takers, not just athletes. The abuse of both legal and illegal drugs can have terrible effects on a person's health. For example, the long-term use of cocaine can lead to a heart attack or **stroke**. Heroin or morphine use can cause infection of the heart lining and valves, liver disease, and fatal overdose. **Hallucinogenic drugs** can lead to **convulsions**, **coma**, and heart and lung failure. Many drugs are also addictive, which means that users become physically dependent on them. They cannot simply stop taking the drugs, even if they want to.

✔ **Poisoned victory**

Drugs in sports are not new. It is thought that athletes in the ancient Olympic Games (at Olympia, in Greece) used stimulating potions to build themselves up. In the third modern Olympics, held in St. Louis, Missouri, in 1904, the **marathon** was won by U.S. athlete Thomas Hicks. But by the time he crossed the line, Hicks was in a total daze because he had taken the poisonous drug strychnine, and several shots of brandy, to help him keep going. Drug tests were introduced into the Olympics only in 1968.

> *Fighting doping*
> Former WADA
> president Dick
> Pound speaks at a
> conference at the
> Olympic Museum
> at Lausanne,
> Switzerland, in 2007.

World Anti-Doping Agency

The World Anti-Doping Agency (WADA) was set up in 1999. It is an independent organization that promotes and monitors what it calls "the fight against doping in sport." WADA is funded by the International Olympic Committee (IOC), governments, and public authorities around the world. Its headquarters are in Montreal, Canada. In January 2004 WADA produced an Anti-Doping Code that was in effect at the Olympic Games in Athens that year.

A former president of WADA, Richard (Dick) Pound, stated:

```
"Advances in scientific research mean that we are
closing the gap on the cheats... In this new era,
it is evident that the public is much less tolerant
of doping and is more aware and concerned about its
dangers and consequences. People understand that what
happens at the elite level of sport has a trickle-
down effect on their children, who want to emulate the
sports stars... The objective, however, remains the
same: to deter doping and to protect clean athletes'
rights to competition that is safe and fair."

[Source: www.wada-ama.org/en/dynamic.ch2?pageCategory.
id=254]
```

WADA's aims are backed by many other international organizations, including the United Nations Educational, Scientific, and Cultural Organization (UNESCO). UNESCO adopted an International Convention Against Doping in Sport, because it was:

"... concerned by the use of doping by athletes in sport and the consequences thereof for their health, the principle of fair play, the elimination of cheating, and the future of sport; mindful also of the influence that elite athletes have on youth."

[Source: http://portal.unesco.org/en/ev.php-URL_ID=31037&URL_DO=DO_TOPIC&URL_SECTION=201.html]

Role models

The statements from WADA and UNESCO both mention the importance of sports stars as influential role models for young people, who may want to emulate, or copy, them. Do you think this is right or fair? Certainly it might influence the punishments that are handed out to guilty drug-abusers, just as a judge might give a criminal a harsh sentence to act as a deterrent, discouraging people from that type of behavior.

✔ Prohibited substances

The WADA list of prohibited substances divides them into four classes:

1. Prohibited at all times, in- and out-of-competition; includes anabolic steroids, growth **hormones**, and **diuretics**.

2. Prohibited in-competition; includes **stimulants** (such as amphetamines), **narcotics** (such as heroin), and marijuana (cannabis).

3. Prohibited in-competition in particular sports, such as alcohol* and **beta blockers**.

4. Specified substances, which may be generally available, especially in medicines.

* In the 2008 WADA list, alcohol is prohibited in-competition by these sports: aeronautics (air sports), archery, billiards, bobsledding, bowls (a lawn sport), curling, gymnastics, modern pentathlon, motor sports (including Formula One and motorcycling), powerboating, sailing, shooting, skiing/snowboarding, and wrestling.

How many positive tests?

In 2006 WADA agencies carried out nearly 200,000 tests, and almost 2 percent of these revealed traces of prohibited substances. That means that nearly 1 in every 50 tests was positive. Sports scientists call these positive tests "adverse analytical findings." They point out that the figures include athletes who had exemption certificates (see page 19) and who had more than one test on the same sample. By contrast in 1993, when tests were carried out by the IOC, only 1.37 percent of the nearly 90,000 tests carried out were positive.

Which drugs are found most?

The drugs most popular with athletes are anabolic agents. They made up nearly half of the positive results in 2006. This table shows which drugs were found, and in what percentages, in the tests with adverse analytical findings.

Substance group	% found in positive tests in 2003	% found in positive tests in 2006
Anabolic agents (e.g., anabolic steroids)	32.1	45.4
Beta-2 agonists (e.g., used to treat asthma)	10.9	14.6
Cannabinoids (e.g., marijuana)	13.9	12.8
Stimulants (e.g., amphetamines)	19.0	11.3
Diuretics and other masking agents (used to hide drug abuse)	5.2	6.7
Glucocorticosteroids (e.g., hydrocortisone)	10.5	6.5
Others	8.4	2.7

[Source: www.wada-ama.org/rtecontent/document/LABSTATS_2006.pdf]

> *Catching cheaters*

Dr. Donald Catlin, director of the drug-testing laboratory at the University of California, developed a chemical test to catch athletes using a steroid called tetrahydrogestrinone (THG).

Anabolic steroids

Anabolic steroids are chemicals produced from the male hormone **testosterone**. Athletes take steroids to increase muscle size, physical strength, and body weight. These steroids are banned by all major sports governing bodies and are controlled drugs in most countries. That is because they have very serious side effects, such as high blood pressure, liver damage, heart problems, and aggressive behavior. In female athletes, anabolic steroids may cause the appearance of male physical characteristics, such as hair on the face. But some athletes are prepared to take the chance. In 1989 Olympic silver medalist sprinter Angella Taylor-Issajenko of Canada confessed to taking a steroid called stanozolol.

> "I came to the conclusion that people I'd compete with in Moscow were also on anabolics, so I decided that was the way to go. People are not concerned with the side effects, or so-called side effects, with anabolic use. They don't believe it. First and foremost what comes to mind is this is going to help me be the best in the world. Whatever comes later, comes later."
>
> [From: David R. Mottram, ed., *Drugs in Sport*, London: Routledge (2005), p. 46.]

Blood and gene doping

Class I of the WADA prohibited list (see page 13) also includes some prohibited methods. The first is **blood doping**, which involves boosting an athlete's red blood cells. Some of the athlete's blood is extracted a few weeks before a competition. It is enriched, then transfused back in before the competition. The enriched blood can carry more oxygen and improve endurance. However, there is an increased risk of heart attack or stroke. **Gene doping** is a more recent development. A form of genetic engineering, it involves the use of genetic material to improve athletic performance. Medical scientists are researching this field to help treat serious diseases. In 2005 WADA President Dick Pound wrote:

> "Gene therapy represents an exciting and promising step forward in medical research, but its use to enhance athletic ability is as wrong as any type of traditional doping... It is hard to conceive what the consequences could be of altering a person's genetic makeup just to make them better in sports. This is a slippery slope we do not ever want to go down."
>
> [Source: www.wada-ama.org/rtecontent/document/Play_True_01_2005_en.pdf]

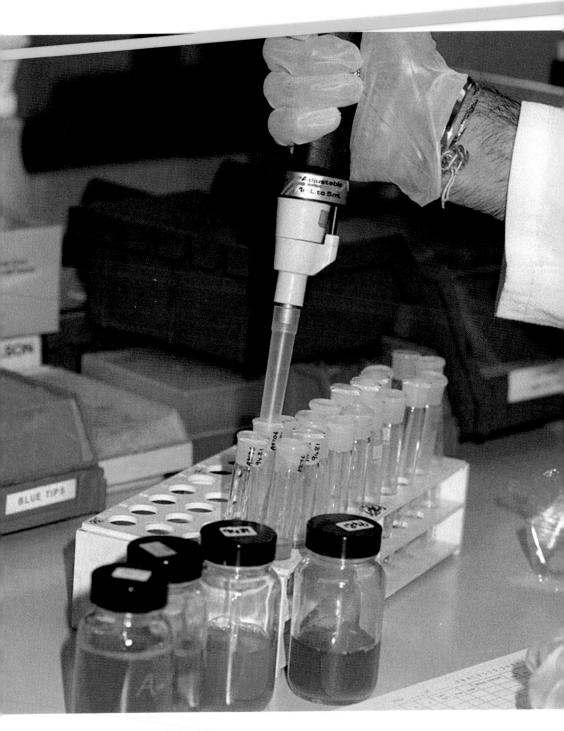

> *High-tech chemistry*

The scientists who work for the anti-doping agencies try
hard to stay one step ahead of drug-using athletes. Most tests
involve checking urine (as shown above), and technicians
have to be very careful not to contaminate the samples.

Tests And Penalties

When drug tests were first introduced in the 1960s, they could detect only a few substances. At first the tests were all carried out during or after competitions. But the authorities realized that drug-using athletes could be using banned substances in training that could not be detected in competition. In 1977 out-of-competition testing was introduced. Since then testing procedures have become much more thorough. But the authorities also try to make sure they are fair and correct. They have to be, because otherwise innocent athletes could be found guilty. A guilty verdict can ruin a sports career. Where there is doubt, the authorities may never know the true answer. Some athletes who have tested positive continue to protest their innocence.

In 1990 U.S. sprinter Butch Reynolds was banned for two years after failing a drug test. However, the U.S. Supreme Court then ruled that there were errors in the testing and insisted that Reynolds be allowed to run in the Olympic trials.

Testing procedures

In most sports, winners are tested along with other competitors. At the control station, selected competitors are asked to fill out forms and declare any medication or other substances taken recently. Then they choose a sealed plastic container for their urine sample. If they feel they cannot produce the sample, they can choose a drink and wait until they are ready.

When the competitor is ready, he or she is accompanied to the bathroom and observed by a sampling officer of the same sex. This is to make sure that this is definitely that person's urine produced at that exact time. At least 2.5 ounces (75 mL) of urine is needed for the test. The competitor then chooses two sealed glass bottles, labeled A and B. He or she pours some of the urine sample into each bottle, and the bottles are then sealed. The bottles have unique numbers or barcodes, and these are put on the competitor's form. A copy of the form is sent with the samples, but without the competitor's name, to the laboratory.

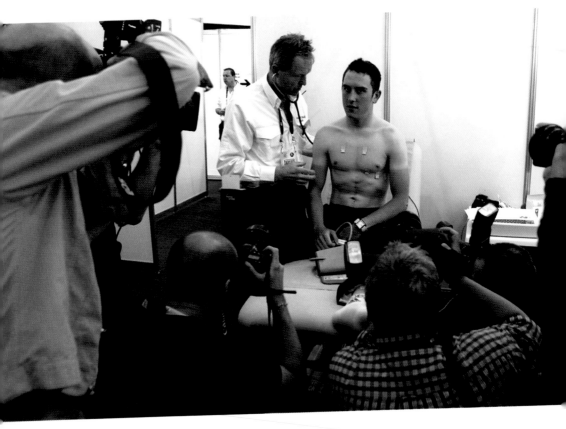

> A check-up before the race

This competitor in the 2007 Tour de France (see pages 33–39) is getting a full medical check before the start of the race, while journalists and photographers look on.

Athletes can apply for a Therapeutic Use Exemption (TUE) certificate, to allow them to use certain prohibited substances. To get the certificate, they must show that there is no alternative medicine, that their health would otherwise be damaged, and that the substance would only return them to a healthy state and not enhance their performance.

At the lab

At the laboratory, the A sample is tested and the B sample is kept in reserve at a constant temperature of 39°F (4°C). The tests are done by sensitive equipment. If they are negative (find nothing), the competitor is informed and the B sample is destroyed. If there is a positive result, the competitor is first invited to explain the finding. Then the B sample is tested by different analysts and in the presence of a sports official and the competitor, if he or she wishes. The analysts look specifically for the prohibited substance found in the A sample. If it is found, the competitor is usually suspended immediately, and a disciplinary hearing is arranged.

✔ Anti-doping workers

At the Salt Lake City Winter Olympics in 2002, the seven paid Olympic anti-doping sample collectors (which excludes the testing laboratory staff) were helped by 390 volunteers, including:

✔ 50 doping control officers to process urine and blood specimens and complete paperwork

✔ 30 site supervisors to run the doping control station

✔ 25 **phlebotomists** to take blood samples*

✔ technical officers to witness urine tests

✔ an escort supervisor, escorts, and couriers.

* The IOC introduced blood-sample tests for skiers at the 1994 Winter Olympics in Lillehammer (in Norway) to detect blood doping. The procedures are similar to urine-sampling, but with just 0.1 ounces (4 mL) of blood split into A and B samples.

Penalties

WADA's Anti-Doping Code lists the following penalties for failing a drug test. Disqualification from the event is followed by:
- First violation: Two-year ban
- Second violation: Lifetime ban.

For a violation involving a "specified substance" (see page 13), which may have been taken unintentionally and was not intended to enhance performance, the bans are:
- First violation: A warning and up to a maximum one-year ban
- Second violation: Two-year ban
- Third violation: Lifetime ban.

In addition, the Olympic Charter states that athletes found guilty of a drug offense at the Olympic Games will have a lifetime ban from the games, even from working as a coach or official.

Individual sports

The U.S. National Football League (NFL), which has tested for steroid abuse since 1987, states as its policy:

"Substance abuse can lead to on-the-field injuries, to alienation of the fans, to diminished job performance, and to personal hardship. The deaths of several NFL players have demonstrated the potentially tragic consequences of substance abuse. NFL players should not by their conduct suggest that substance abuse is either acceptable or safe."

[Source: http://news.findlaw.com/legalnews/sports/drugs/policy/football]

The NFL's penalties for violations are:
- First violation: Banned for four games (a quarter of a regular season)
- Second violation: Banned for eight games
- Third violation: Banned for one year.

U.S. Major League Baseball only started testing for drugs in 2002 and finally introduced penalties in 2005. These have since been made tougher and are:
- First violation: Banned for 50 games (a third of a season)
- Second violation: Banned for 100 games
- Third violation: Lifetime ban.

Rule changes

Just as individual sports change their doping rules, so too does WADA, as scientists make new findings about individual drugs. A good example is caffeine, which is found in coffee, tea, and many sodas. Caffeine used to be on the IOC banned list, but was removed by WADA in 2004. This was because caffeine beverages are commonly enjoyed, and scientists said that its physical effects were minimal. However, some athletes have found that caffeine improves their performance when taken in large doses as tablets or injections. In 2005 the Australian rugby union player George Gregan said that caffeine pills boosted his performance by 7 percent. WADA has placed the drug on a monitoring list. It is tested for, and results are kept of its use to help officials decide in the future whether or not it should be prohibited.

> *Coffee break*
Hawthorn Hawks Australian-Rules Football team
members relax at a training camp with cups of coffee.

Marijuana is a drug made from the hemp plant. It is usually smoked or mixed with food or drink. Its use is illegal in most countries for all citizens. Since it is unlikely that it would be used to improve performance, it was not originally on many banned lists. In 1998 the Canadian snowboarder Ross Rebagliati tested positive for marijuana and was stripped of his Olympic gold medal. Then the IOC realized that the International Ski Federation had different rules, and Rebagliati got his medal back. He claimed that the result must have come from second-hand smoke (smoke from others). Since 2004 marijuana has been on the WADA prohibited list because it is seen as a health risk.

> *From silver to disqualification*

Bulgarian weightlifter Ivan Ivanov won silver
in the Olympic 56-kilogram (123-pound)
event at Sydney in 2000. He was then
disqualified after testing positive for a banned
drug called furosemide.

One Rule For All?

Should the drug rules be exactly the same for all sports? WADA thinks so, and is trying to be consistent across the sports world. Many people think this makes sense, because it treats all athletes the same. Shouldn't a baseball player be treated in the same way as a sprinter?

Most high-level athletes take part in professional rather than amateur sports, so sports are their livelihood. Does this make a difference? Is it right that an athlete is banned for life for taking a substance that is allowed to other people? In Mexico, anabolic steroids are not controlled in general use, and in other countries they can be prescribed by doctors. So, an accountant, for example, could use drugs to improve his performance in his job, but a weightlifter could not.

In 2000 Bulgaria's entire weightlifting team was thrown out of the Olympic Games in Sydney. Three medalists tested positive for a diuretic substance, and the International Weightlifting Federation applied the sanction under its "three strikes and out" rule. This means that a national federation is suspended for at least 12 months if three of its lifters test positive in one year.

How do various sports compare in terms of drug offenses? Those on the chart below were the most offending Olympic sports in 2006. The worst offender was cycling, the sport that most brought the drug problem to the attention of the sports world (see pages 33–39).

Sport	Samples analyzed in 2006	Adverse analytical findings in 2006	% positive in 2006	% positive in 2003
Cycling	14,229	594	4.17	3.93
Weightlifting	6,543	187	2.86	2.06
Triathlon	2,366	67	2.83	1.38
Boxing	2,553	61	2.39	3.68
Baseball	15.977	370	2.32	2.47
Modern pentathlon	480	10	2.08	0.56
Handball	2,568	51	1.99	1.46
Skiing	3,901	76	1.95	1.08
Biathlon	1,094	21	1.92	0.45
Wrestling	3,055	58	1.90	1.73
All Olympic sports	156,866	2,915	1.86	1.51

What about public opinion?

In August 2007 the San Francisco Giants left fielder Barry Bonds beat the all-time Major League Baseball home run record with a total of 756. But many people feel Bonds does not deserve the record, because he has been accused of taking steroids in the past. This has ruined his reputation. How much does that matter? Do you agree with the opinion of this journalist?

Bonds's Future Is on the Line, But His Past Is in the Way

Barry Bonds has worked for years to construct his reputation as the surly superstar, a man who cares so little about public opinion that he could barely face a television camera without sneering... Rehabilitating his reputation, several experts say, will require two things: an admission he took steroids and an apology. "There's a big difference between a court of law and the court of public opinion," said Mike Paul, the president of MGP & Associates PR in New York. "I'm sure an attorney is telling him, 'You can't say you're sorry or that you took steroids,' but it's the only thing that would repair his reputation." ... "What Barry doesn't realize is, the court of opinion is really the court of life," said Paul, who cited as an example the fallout over the O. J. Simpson trial. "He wasn't convicted, but everyone knows what happened in the court of public opinion."

[By Lynn Zinser, *New York Times*, August 12, 2007.]

Government-sponsored cheating

"How does a country of fewer than 17 million people double its Olympic output from 20 to 40 gold medals in just four years? Drugs, and plenty of 'em." That, according to the CBC Sports Canada website, is how the former East Germany became a sporting giant in the 1970s and 1980s. Apparently, many of the country's athletes thought what they were being given were vitamins, when in fact they were anabolic steroids and other drugs. In 2007 the German Athletics Federation was criticized for nominating a former Olympic champion, Heike Drechsler, for election to the IAAF committee. In 2001 Drechsler admitted that she had unknowingly been part of the East German doping program. She was later let off, like all her country's athletes, because it was decided the drugs had been controlled and issued by the state rather than individual athletes, who thought they were vitamins. Despite the criticism, Drechsler was voted on to the committee.

> *Top long-jumper*

Heike Drechsler won world championships for East Germany before gaining two Olympic gold medals for unified Germany in 1992 and 2000.

> *Checking the small print*

When they buy medicine at a pharmacy or in a supermarket, athletes have to look carefully at the listed ingredients. They must check with the sports authorities if they are in any doubt, so that there is no risk of them taking a banned substance. The experts are there to help.

Accidentally On Purpose?

In almost all cases of positive drug tests, the athletes concerned claim that the test result must be wrong, that their sample must have been tampered with, or that they took the substance without knowing it. This is one reason why some people think that a lifetime ban is always too harsh a punishment, even for a second offense. Most athletes would claim boldly that both positive tests were wrong!

WADA, the IOC, and many sports governing bodies run education programs aimed directly at athletes, so that they are fully aware of the issues involved and can avoid being found out "unknowingly." One of WADA's stated priorities is "leading and coordinating effective doping prevention strategies and education, assisting in the implementation of anti-doping education programs." The idea is that athletes will learn to make fewer silly mistakes and will know and accept that they will not get away with making mistakes.

Another problem is that athletes sometimes miss out-of-competition drug tests. They may claim that they forgot, that they went to the wrong place, or give lots of other excuses. You could make a case that if the authorities accepted these stories, drug-using athletes would soon miss all their test appointments. Sadly, the real drug users make life very difficult for the clean athletes.

Should drugs never be used in sports?

"Although there may be many reasons why athletes use drugs, four main reasons can be identified:
- Legitimate therapeutic use (prescription drug or self-medication)
- Performance continuation (treatment of sports injuries)
- Recreational/social use (legal and illegal)
- Performance enhancement.
In each of the above categories there are drugs that appear in the WADA list of banned substances.

"Inevitably, clear distinctions cannot always be made between these uses. It would be easy to say that athletes should avoid taking drugs, for any reason, particularly at the time of a competition. However, there are many circumstances when drug taking is advisable, if not imperative, for the general health and well-being of the athlete. Therefore it would be prudent for athletes to consider the specific need for taking drugs and the full implications of their action."

[From David R. Mottram, ed., *Drugs in Sport*, London: Routledge (2005), p. 20.]

David Mottram is a pharmacist and an expert on drug abuse in sports. Do you agree that he has painted a balanced picture of why athletes might take drugs? His is a useful explanation, because many people might think athletes should simply never take any drugs at all, because then there would be no problem.

✔ Nutritional supplements

David Mottram also issues a warning about supplements. Vitamin preparations and **nutritional supplements** might contain banned substances that are not listed on the package, so they should be avoided. Athletes also take sports drinks that contain carbohydrates, to provide energy, and **electrolytes**, to help control fluid balance in the body. As with other products, athletes must know what they are taking. If in doubt, they should ask a specialist.

Asthma

Exercise can sometimes trigger asthma and cause breathing difficulties in athletes, but some drugs used to combat asthma contain banned substances. Athletes with asthma can obtain an exemption certificate in order to take medicines that are banned for other athletes. Unscrupulous athletes could therefore pretend to have asthma.

In 2003 Argentinian tennis player Mariano Puerta was banned for two years after testing positive for an anabolic substance, which he said had been taken to treat asthma. The ban was reduced to nine months, but two years later Puerta tested positive for a stimulant. He was banned for eight years, despite claiming that tiny amounts of the drug had been accidentally left by his wife in a glass. The ban was later reduced to two years by the Court of **Arbitration** for Sport, and Puerta is now playing again.

> *French runner-up*
>
> **Mariano Puerta of Argentina lost the 2005 French Open tennis final to Rafael Nadal of Spain before being banned for using drugs.**

Mistakes, mistakes

What if an athlete makes a genuine mistake? There have been many cases in which athletes' stories were believed, but they were still found guilty. In 2002 British skier Alain Baxter won an Olympic bronze medal at Salt Lake City. He then tested positive for methamphetamine. This came from a nasal decongestant inhaler that he bought in the United States. Baxter had assumed this was the same as the British version of the same brand of inhaler, which does not contain methamphetamine, but it was not. Baxter did not check the inhaler's list of ingredients or show it to a medical expert. He thought it was the same as inhalers he had used safely before.

The IOC stripped Baxter of his medal. The International Ski Federation accepted that it was a genuine mistake and banned him for three months. Baxter appealed, pointing out that the substance did not improve his performance. The ban was lifted, but his medal was not returned. If you take the view that "rules are rules," you might think the treatment of Baxter was fair, even though he made an innocent mistake. He learned the hard way that athletes must check and declare every chemical substance they take.

✔ What do they think?

"If athletes are serious about their sport and their career, they should be more careful than to just accidentally take a banned substance. But mistakes are often made, and if it is clear that it was merely an act of momentary mindlessness, then a penalty should not be enforced."

Georgia, 20, a student

Missed tests

There have been several well-publicized cases in recent years of athletes missing out-of-competition drug tests. The authorities feel they must be tough on this, because otherwise drug abusers will continue doing it. But who is to say if the athletes are telling the truth? Just before the 2004 Olympics in Athens, Greek sprinter Konstantinos Kenteris and his training partner, Ekaterini Thanou, failed to attend a drug test. They claimed they were injured in a motorcycle accident, and later Kenteris insisted he had not been asked to take a test. After a hearing before the Disciplinary Commission of the IOC, the sprinters withdrew from the games. An official investigation found that their accident had been staged, and they had also missed two tests earlier in the year. They were banned for two years.

> *IOC hearing*

Sprinter Konstantinos Kenteris was the center of attention when he attended an IOC hearing in Athens before he withdrew from the 2004 games. Having won the 100-meter gold four years earlier in Sydney, the Greek athlete was a favorite to win with the home crowds.

British 400-meter runner Christine Ohuruogu missed three out-of-competition drug tests in 2005–06. She was banned for a year, and the British Olympic Association banned her from all future Olympic Games. Ohuruogu appealed successfully against the Olympic ban. In a newspaper poll, 62 percent of respondents thought she should be allowed to run in the 2008 Olympics (with 38 percent against). After returning to the track, Ohuruogu won the 400-meters gold medal at the 2007 World Championships in Osaka.

Even the WADA president said he had "legal sympathy" for Ohuruogu. After all, she never tested positive, including in tests carried out soon after the missed tests. Athletes have to declare where they will be most of the time, so they can be tested, but this can be difficult if their schedules change unexpectedly. Should they be penalized for this?

> *Racing its reputation downhill*

Tour de France riders race down a pass in the
Pyrenees Mountains during a 2006 stage of the
event. Experts agree that the tour is one of the
world's toughest sporting challenges, but drug
scandals have tarnished its image. Is its reputation
ruined, or does this great event still have a future?

Case Study: The Tour De France

People call the Tour de France cycle race the largest annual sporting event in the world. It is certainly one of the most physically demanding events, and it is also very popular with spectators. Between 175 and 200 of the world's top professional cyclists cover around 2,175 miles (3,500 kilometers) in 21 stages, spread out over three weeks every July. The cyclists ride around France and sometimes cross into neighboring countries. The toughest stages include steep climbs in the Alps and Pyrenees mountains. There are also races through flat countryside and individual time trials. The race always finishes in Paris.

The racing teams are generally financed by large businesses in exchange for lots of publicity. The overall race leader is identified by wearing a yellow jersey. The tour makes great demands on the cyclists' strength and stamina, since they race almost every day with very few rest days.

In recent years, the tour has been dogged by doping scandals. In 2006 the winner was disqualified (see page 37). The situation has become so bad that some people say the future of the race is in doubt. In 2007, after more drug problems, the president of the International Cycling Union (UCI) called for a lifetime ban for first-time offenders.

Tour beginnings

The first Tour de France took place in 1903, and early riders drank brandy and inhaled **ether** to dull their senses and kill the pain of competing in the race. In the first half of the 20th century, people saw nothing wrong with this, and riders probably started taking other drugs to improve their performance. Those who did not do so must have realized they were at a disadvantage in such a grueling competition.

> *In the Alps*

A steep climb in the 2007 tour is led by Carlos Sastre of Spain.

Realizing the dangers

The terrible dangers of taking drugs on the tour were first realized in 1967, when British cyclist Tom Simpson died on the steep climb of Mont Ventoux, a 6,263-foot- (1,909-meter-) high peak in southern France. Simpson began weaving across the road, then collapsed near the summit. He died of a heart attack. Amphetamines were later discovered in his bloodstream.

The UCI applied its first sanctions in that same year, handing out fines and up to three-month suspensions to riders who took drugs or refused to take tests. It then made this appeal:

"We hereby want to launch an alarm call to national governments, to urge them to institute, without delay, strict controls over the distribution, sale, and use of doping agents. Radical measures in this field would undoubtedly prevent the massive circulation of these deadly products, which some believe to have miraculous powers, and whose only qualities are those of destruction. We are convinced that this appeal will be heard and that with such support, we will succeed in eliminating this evil, veritable scourge for athletes."

[Source: www.uci.ch/templates/UCI/UCI5/layout. asp?MenuId=MjI0NQ link: 40 years fighting against doping]

> *Tom Simpson*

Riders view a memorial at Mont Ventoux to Tom Simpson, which marks where he died during the 1967 tour.

Fighting a losing battle?

In 1981 Prince Alexandre de Mérode, president of the IOC Medical Commission, said cycling was an example for all international sports federations, since the UCI was leading the battle against doping. In 1991 the UCI used the motto, "Doping puts riders' lives in danger." The UCI then had two major concerns: riders' health and sports ethics, which it called "fairness and respect." In 1992 the UCI founded an Anti-Doping Commission. This stressed the need to influence everyone who in turn had control over the riders: team managers, coaches, doctors, parents, and friends. They were on the right track, but there were still drug problems, and they were getting worse.

The "Tour of Shame"

The drug issue exploded during the 1998 Tour de France. A healthcare assistant for one of the teams was arrested when EPO (see opposite), amphetamines, testosterone, and growth hormones were found in his car. French police found more drugs in raids on several other team hotels. Some teams left the tour, and riders staged a sit-down strike. Only 96 out of 189 riders finished what some newspapers called the "Tour de Dopage" (Tour of Doping) or "Tour of Shame."

> Drug arrest

Cristian Moreni of Italy was arrested by French police after failing a drug test in the 2007 race (see page 38). Moreni admitted his guilt.

Guilty or not guilty?

The 1998 tour was won by Marco Pantani of Italy, who failed a blood test in a different event the following year and was accused of drug offenses. The 1999 winner, Lance Armstrong of the United States, went on to win the tour a record seven times . . . in a row! This was an amazing achievement and, given the state of the sport, it was inevitable that allegations would be made against him.

Armstrong completely denied all the accusations. He called himself "the most tested athlete in the world," yet only once in his career did a prohibited substance show up in his urine. This was a small amount of an anti-inflammatory drug, outside the positive range, for which he had a medical certificate to show that it was in an approved cream that he used for saddle sores. There was a campaign against him, and you might take the view that "there's no smoke without fire." But is this right? Shouldn't these athletes only be judged strictly by the facts—that is, by the results of scientific tests?

In the United States, people questioned the testing methods. They also wondered if there was an anti-American campaign because of Armstrong's domination of the tour. Some people doubt the honesty of athletes, but many others have little faith in the tests and testing organizations.

✔ EPO blood boosting

In the 1980s, a new form of blood doping (see page 15) was developed. This involved injecting a synthetic form of the hormone erythropoietin (EPO), which regulates the production of red blood cells. The drug was developed to treat patients with cancer and kidney disease. In healthy people, too much EPO can cause heart failure, yet athletes continue to take it. Until 2000 it was difficult to tell natural from injected EPO in a test. But in 2000 WADA approved a new system that could do this, though some people doubt its accuracy and say it could give false results. The authorities believe that EPO is used widely in endurance sports. In 2007 the 1996 Tour de France winner, Bjarne Riis of Denmark, admitted to taking EPO during his career. The UCI has asked him to return his yellow winner's jersey.

Going by the book

After he won the 2006 tour, U.S. cyclist Floyd Landis was found to have failed a test for testosterone on the 17th stage. His case was referred to the UCI, USA Cycling, and the U.S. Anti-Doping Agency, and then finally to an arbitration panel. Eventually, Landis was stripped of his title and banned for two years. He continues to insist he is innocent and has said, "I would advise athletes all over the world to stop giving urine samples until these guys clean up their act."

More bad publicity

The 2007 Tour de France brought more bad publicity. Alexander Vinokourov of Kazakhstan tested positive for blood doping, so his team pulled out of the race. Next, Cristian Moreni of Italy tested positive for testosterone, and his team pulled out. Finally, tour leader and favorite to win, Michael Rasmussen of Denmark, was taken out of the race by his team for "violating team rules" before the tour (though his drug tests during the tour were negative). The race was eventually won by Alberto Contador of Spain.

The French press decided enough was enough. *France Soir* said the tour had died at the age of 104, after a long illness. "The tour is clinically dead. It is a broken toy, a burst soap bubble popped by careless kids, unaware that they are damaging themselves, their health, and their childhood dreams as well." Media around the world agreed. *USA Today* suggested that cycling was in such a bad state that it might lose its Olympic status.

> *A troubled tour*

Michael Rasmussen (Denmark) wears the race leader's yellow jersey during the ninth stage of the 2007 tour. After the 16th stage, Rasmussen was withdrawn from the race by his team.

Doping Issues Have Cycling Facing Uncertain Future

Alberto Contador's final-weekend ascension to Tour de France champion gave the world's biggest cycling race a moment of grace after a series of doping scandals marred the event, but today professional cycling continues with its future very much in doubt. The international cycling federation (UCI) and the organizers of the three Grand Tours of France, Italy, and Spain can't agree on how the war on doping should be fought. At the Olympic level, illegal doping by professionals threatens to endanger the sport's status in the Summer Games. "If cycling doesn't resolve this problem, I'd go so far as saying it should be excluded from the Olympics," International Olympic Committee member Rene Fasel of Switzerland told the Associated Press. "Just tell them 'no more.' It's discrediting all those who are honest and clean. The heads of cycling need to know that if they don't clean up the sport, and really clean it up, then it's goodbye."

[By Sal Ruibal, *USA Today*, July 29, 2007. www.usatoday.com/sports/cycling/tourdefrance/2007-07-29-future-doping_N.htm]

Who is to blame?

Who do you think is most to blame for this complicated situation? Is it the cycling governing body (UCI), the organizers of the tour (Amaury Sport), the cycling teams, or the riders themselves? Or perhaps all of them? The riders and teams are under great pressure to win, given the huge amounts of money available from sponsors. Yet the sponsoring companies care about their reputations, so they should be firmly against doping. This applies to the organizers and the governing body, too, but they are also very eager to keep the sport going.

✔ Signing up for fines

Would huge fines for drug offenders work as well as bans? Certainly some riders do not like the idea of them. In 2007 the world road-race champion, Olympic gold medalist, and Tour de France stage winner, Paolo Bettini of Italy, refused to sign the anti-doping charter. He did not agree that riders should pay a fine of a year's income for failing a drug test. The host city of the 2007 World Road Championship, Stuttgart in Germany, wanted Bettini banned from the race for not signing up, but they failed to do so. Bettini won the race and retained his title.

> *Making their point*

At the 2001 World Championships in Edmonton, Canada, British runners Hayley Tullett (left) and Paula Radcliffe made their feelings known. They were protesting because Russian Olga Yegorova was allowed to run despite having tested positive for EPO. She went on to win gold in the 5,000 meters.

For And Against

You can see from many of the case studies and quotations in this book that people have extreme views on the issue of how to deal with drugs in sports. We are mainly dealing here with professional sports, and especially the top performers in their particular sport, because they have the greatest incentive to win—the chance to earn very large sums of money.

Nevertheless, most competitors and spectators realize that, without the element of fair competition, sports could be seen as meaningless. This is shown by attendance figures at so-called friendly competitions. People are less interested in matches where there is nothing at stake. Many professional sports rely on entertaining the spectators, because they are the ones who ultimately pay the athletes' salaries. But to many spectators the entertainment comes from watching top athletes compete against each other, without any unfair advantage to anyone.

According to the Olympic Charter, sports must recognize "the educational value of good example and respect for universal fundamental ethical principles," and support "the preservation of human dignity." Every individual should have the opportunity to play sports without discrimination of any kind, and "with a spirit of friendship, solidarity, and fair play." Do drug-using athletes ruin "fair play," and should they therefore be treated severely?

Taking a stand

Many athletes and retired sports heroes feel very strongly that they and current clean athletes must stand up and speak out against doping. U.S. Olympic gold medalist Ed Moses helped to set up a pioneering out-of-competition drug testing program. He believes passionately that drug-using athletes should be dealt with firmly. Moses was himself an amazing athlete. He broke the 400-meter hurdles world record four times, and over a period of 10 years won 122 races, including 107 finals, in a row. This is what he had to say in 2007:

```
Time to Take a Stand Against the Cheats
and the Spineless

Over the last two years I have watched in disgust as
more and more "name brand" athletes have become ensnared
in the omnipresent net that we have come to know as
"testing positive" for performance-enhancing drugs.
Whether each athlete implicated is guilty or not, the
names form an embarrassing Who's Who in the world of
sport... It is now time for me, and for other clean,
world-class athletes from every sport, to speak out
loudly against the claim that doping is simply "the
way it is" and the only way to the top... To reach the
pinnacle of my event, the 400 meters hurdles—and to
stay there without ceding victory, as I did, for nearly
a decade—I did not need or want to use performance-
enhancing drugs... By definition, the elite level of
sport is not open to just anyone. Only the very rare
individual will succeed. But to suggest that drugs are a
de facto key to one, two, or more world-class victories
is a lie.

[By Ed Moses, The Times, May 21, 2007.
www.timesonline.co.uk/tol/sport/more_sport/
article1816380.ece]
```

✔ What do they think?

"If you're going to impose a rigorous set of rules for one sport, then it should be the same for all professional athletes alike. If they are all being paid, then it follows that they should all be held similarly accountable."

Georgia, 20, a student

> *High impact*

Players in high-impact, aggressive sports, such as football, may be more tempted to take drugs. Currently, National Football League (NFL) drug penalties are not as severe as those imposed by many other sports governing bodies.

For the life ban

Many current and former athletes are on record as saying that they support a life ban for drug offenses. Some even suggest that this ultimate sanction should be brought in for first offenses. Sebastian Coe, vice-president of the IAAF, said in 2007 that if athletes set out to cheat, they have no place in sports. Commenting on the case of a particular sprinter who had just received a two-year ban, Coe said that in his opinion the athlete should never be allowed to come back.

Michele Verroken, the head of a sports consultancy and an anti-doping campaigner, wrote in an article that the very future of sports is at risk. She supports clean athletes and condemns dopers (or "dopes" as she calls them):

```
"Athletes themselves must be part of the fight back. If
the majority of athletes are calling for life bans for
those who are doping and defrauding them of sporting
success, why are they being denied that protection?
... Rather than justifying their drug habit or boring
us with their 'extenuating circumstances,' where is the
honest admission from those dopes that they were just
not good enough?"

[Source: www.sundayherald.com/sport/nationalsport/
display.var.1596597.0.the_future_of_the_sport_is_at_
risk.php]
```

To cheat or not to cheat?

Victor Conte was the founder of the Bay Area Laboratory Co-Operative (BALCO), a California-based company that was involved in a huge drug scandal. This had huge implications, because athletes from around the world had been trained and guided by coaches involved in the scandal. Conte has claimed that there is a "use-or-lose" mentality among athletes: If you don't use drugs, you will lose races or games. This article followed a TV interview with Conte. What do you think of his views?

How Drugs Shattered America's Olympic Dreams

In a single television interview, one man has blown apart the myths and legends of world sporting achievement. When Victor Conte sat down with celebrity TV interviewer Martin Bashir he was dressed simply in a white shirt... "The Olympic Games are a fraud. The whole history of the Games is just full of corruption, cover-up, performance-enhancing drug use. It's not what the world thinks it is." ... He insisted in his interview, drugs had been in sport so long and been used so prevalently that the "playing field" was still level. It was confirmation of the cynical joke about the Olympics—it was now a race between chemists, not athletes ... Conte said: "It's not cheating if everybody is doing it. And if you've got the knowledge that that's what everyone is doing, and those are the real rules of the game, then you're not cheating."

[By Paul Harris and Denis Campbell, *Observer*, December 5, 2004. http://sport.guardian.co.uk/news/story/0,10488,1366955,00.html. Copyright Guardian News and Media 2004.]

He is saying that you are just cheating yourself if you do not take drugs, because you have less chance of winning. This cynical view ignores fair play and the health risks of drugs. It is like saying there are thieves in our society, so we should all steal things—otherwise they will have more than us and that is not fair. What do you think of this argument? If winning means so much to athletes that they are prepared to forget everything else, perhaps this is the problem that needs to be fixed. Do you agree?

An extreme pro-drugs view is that we will never be able to stop athletes from taking drugs, so we should simply let them take all the drugs they want. For example, Tony Millar of the Lewisham Sports Medicine Clinic in Australia believes that anabolic steroids should be openly prescribed to athletes.

> *Marion Jones*

U.S. sprinter Marion Jones won five medals at the 2000 Olympics. But in 2007 she admitted that she had taken steroids, and so the medals were taken away. In 2008 she was sentenced to six months in prison for lying in a court of law.

Avoiding mistakes

Is the current situation reasonable as long as the testing methods are reliable? Will this ever be possible? Is the key issue the penalty given for a second offense? Some people have lost faith in the tests and testers, even though drug testing laboratories very rarely make errors. Perhaps there should be three tests or more. How could we make the testing system even more reliable?

Anyone can make a mistake—miss a test or accidentally take a prohibited substance—but this really should not happen twice. One view is that we should accept there will be occasional mistakes in banning someone innocent, but if athletes have two chances, this is a risk worth taking to combat the real drug users. Or perhaps this view is unacceptable, when there is so much at stake for individual athletes. What do you think?

✔ What do they think?

"I think the penalties of a two-year ban for a first offense and a life ban for a second offense are about right. At least it gives them a chance to redeem themselves after their first offense, but a life ban is appropriate for disobeying the rules again."

Oliver, 15, a student

"I think the penalties are too lenient—there should be no second chance. If athletes knowingly take such performance-enhancing drugs, they are arrogantly showing no respect to the sport or to themselves."

Georgia, 20, a student

> *Spectator fun*

Many people enjoy participating in sports, and many also enjoy being spectators. But is the enjoyment spoiled if some athletes gain advantages from drug abuse?

Join The Debate

The central question of this book has been: Should substance-using athletes be banned for life? After all you have read, you should be able to give an informed answer to that question. As part of that answer, you will need to question your own opinions about drug abuse in sports.

To make an overall decision, you need to decide about each of the different issues in this book. Then, you could give each of them a level of significance. An issue can be significant in one of two different ways. It can have quantitative significance, which means that it affects a lot of people. It can also have qualitative significance, meaning that it affects fewer people, but in a serious way.

Substances, such as caffeine, affect many athletes, so their use has a lot of quantitative significance. But the effect is small, so this issue has less qualitative significance. On the other hand, the abuse of anabolic steroids has a lot of qualitative significance for the issue we are discussing, but the number of abusers is relatively small, so it has less quantitative significance.

Issues to think about

Many aspects of the issue of substance-using athletes are covered in this book. Here are some of the questions raised by them:

- Is doping against fair play and the spirit of sports?
- How important are the health issues?
- Are top athletes seen as role models by young people?
- Should there be more or fewer classes of prohibited substances?
- Is it right that blood and gene doping are banned?
- Are the testing procedures reliable enough?
- Are the WADA penalties too soft or too severe?
- Should a lifetime ban come after the first, second, or third violation? Or never?
- Should the penalties be exactly the same in all sports?
- Should a missed test be treated as seriously as a failed test?
- Should an innocent mistake be punished severely? Or is there no such thing as an innocent mistake?
- How effective are fines for substance-using athletes?
- Do all athletes need to take drugs to win just because some do?

Organizing your own debate

A debate is a formal discussion of a topic. It is a good way to examine issues on that topic. A debate may take the form of a question, such as the title of this book, "Should substance-using athletes be banned for life?" It may also be in the form of a **proposition**, which is put in the form of a statement—for example, "Substance-using athletes should be banned for life." People involved in the debate may answer the question in the affirmative or in the negative, or argue in favor of the proposition or against it.

In some debating formats, those involved may take another position entirely. They might reach the conclusion that "maybe" or "in some cases" is better than a straightforward "yes" or "no." On the issue of substance-using athletes, this might refer to imposing a life ban only for a second offense. At one end of the spectrum, speakers might propose that the ban should be imposed immediately for a first offense. Others might suggest that substance-using athletes should be given many more chances.

There are many different ways to organize a debate. A few different formats are suggested here. Make sure, when you debate, that you make complete arguments. Be careful also to refute your opponent's arguments—that is, to show how and why they are wrong. Each of the following debating formats has a set of rules, which you can alter according to the number of participants and the amount of time you have available for the debate.

Two-sided debate

In a two-sided debate, one side (or team) makes a case for the proposition. The other side argues against it. The side arguing for the proposition is called the affirmative. The other side is called the **opposition** or the negative. The first speaker on each side makes a speech. The debate then continues with alternate speakers from each side. The affirmative team, which must try to show that the proposition is more likely to be true, speaks first and last. The opening affirmative speaker makes a case. The first opposition speaker refutes the case. Second speakers continue with their team's points and refute new points from the other side. The final speeches are summaries of the best arguments for a team and the best **refutation** against the major points of the other side. With six students, you could have the following format and speaker times:

1st speaker, affirmative: 5 minutes
1st speaker, opposition: 5 minutes
2nd speaker, affirmative: 5 minutes
2nd speaker, opposition: 5 minutes
3rd speaker, opposition: 3 minutes
3rd speaker, affirmative: 3 minutes

You could add time for questions and comments from the class or audience during, in between, or after speeches.

> *Formal debates*

This formal debate is taking place in an auditorium in front of a large audience. Debates of this type are often part of debating competitions.

Panel discussion

A group of students can participate in a panel discussion on an issue. Students speak for themselves and may agree or disagree with the opinions of others on the panel. The discussion is designed to inform an audience. There should be an overall time limit—for example, 30 minutes—for the entire discussion. You can use a moderator to ask questions and keep the discussion moving. A panel discussion is an opportunity to use conversation in a way that presents and challenges ideas. Audience questions may be added after the discussion.

Open forum

This is an effective format for a class or large group. A single moderator leads an open discussion on a range of topics related to an issue. Members of the audience may present new ideas, add to the presentations from others, or refute any argument. Like brainstorming (group discussions used to produce ideas), this format quickly gets a variety of ideas into a discussion. You could allow an individual or a small panel to judge a debate, voting on the outcome. For larger discussions, you could ask an audience which speaker did best and why.

Preparing your speech

Debaters may read out a written speech, which can be a good idea if you are nervous and worried that you will forget what you meant to say. You can speak from an outline or series of notes, to which you refer as a reminder. This can sound more natural, but has the disadvantage that you might lose your thread or go off the point. If you want to work from notes, it is still a good idea to practice what you might say first. The third way is an impromptu speech, which is completely unprepared and unrehearsed. This is not a good idea for those taking part in a formal debate, though it is a useful skill for members of the audience when they can make comments or ask questions.

Speaking to an audience

Good preparation will make you more confident about what you want to say. Listeners will be more impressed by a positive delivery. When making your speech, relax, breathe normally, and stand up straight and still. Look up from your notes as often as possible, and make eye contact with individual listeners.

Speak loudly and clearly in your natural voice. Emphasize the important words and phrases in your speech. This aids understanding and helps to vary the pitch of your voice, which makes the speech more interesting. Above all, try not to rush. Take your time and express your point of view clearly and confidently.

> *Well done!*
>
> **Many people are nervous about speaking in front of an audience, but careful research and thoughtful preparation can make it fun and informative for everyone involved.**

All opinions count

For many of the issues covered in this book, you have read two or more varying points of view. It is important to remember that to reach an informed, balanced, unbiased view, you must take all these opinions into account. Do not dismiss right away those opinions with which you disagree. Instead, ask yourself why you disagree with them and present a good argument against them. You will then be in a much stronger position to convince others of your views. So, what do you think? Should substance-using athletes be banned for life?

Find Out More

Projects

Carry out your own research on some of the topics covered in this book.

- **Gene doping**
  This is included in the prohibited methods listed by WADA (see page 13). You could begin by typing "gene doping" into an Internet search engine and following the links to newspaper and journal articles. How do you think gene doping compares with blood doping?

- **Individual sports**
  You could research the situation in individual sports not covered in this book. A good starting point would be golf, a sport that has just introduced drug testing and that has begun an educational program for golfers. In 2007 golfing legend Gary Player suggested that golfers were doping. See www.golf.com/golf/tours_news/article/0,28136,1644553,00.html. Do you think it was right that Player spoke out without naming actual offenders?

- **Individual athletes**
  You could look at the cases of individuals and make up your own mind about them. One example could be the former U.S. sprinter Butch Reynolds (see page 17), whose lifted ban brought the U.S. Supreme Court into conflict with the IOC. Other examples are baseball player Barry Bonds (see page 24) and sprinter Marion Jones (see page 45).

- **Asthma and other ailments**
  Many athletes claim to suffer from asthma and other ailments (see page 29). Do you think the rules should be relaxed to help them, or are some of these athletes lying? Look at books and websites before making up your mind. Does the exemption certificate system work?

- **Tour de France**
  There are many books on the doping scandals in the tour, such as David Walsh, *From Lance to Landis: Inside the American Doping Controversy at the Tour de France,* New York: Ballantine (2007). What does the past teach us, and what does the future hold for the tour?

Websites

- **www.wada-ama.org**
  The website of the World Anti-Doping Agency has links to the latest Prohibited List and Anti-Doping Code. You can also read about the agency's mission, priorities, and plans for the future. Try WADA's online doping quiz and see how many you get right. What do you think of the agency's equals-sign logo and their tag line, "Play true"? Do you think they will help prevent cheating? How would you design a logo to do this?

- **www.olympic.org**
  This is the official website of the Olympic movement, putting forward the views of the International Olympic Committee. There is a link to the full text of the Olympic Charter, which gives interesting views on the nature and values of Olympic sports.

- **www.usantidoping.org**
  The very informative website of the U.S. Anti-Doping Agency is dedicated "to preserving the well-being of Olympic sport, the integrity of competition, and ensuring the health of athletes." The site includes a link to Drug Reference Online, which provides easily accessible information on whether specific pharmaceutical products are allowed for use by athletes (including some over-the-counter medicines). A section on "cheating your health" describes the risks involved in taking drugs.

- **www.cbc.ca/sports/indepth/drugs/stories/top10.html**
  CBC Sport Canada has put together a list of ten of the "most influential—and bizarre—drug cases in the past few decades." Some of these cases are covered in this book; others are interesting additions. The cases are written in a dramatic way. Which one do you think is the most scandalous?

Glossary

anabolic steroid — synthetic hormone that, among other effects, increases the size and strength of muscles

arbitration — settlement of disputes by referring them to an expert individual or body

beta blocker — drug that relieves stress on the heart

bias — unfair preference for or against something or someone; a prejudice

blood doping — boosting a person's red blood cells

coma — prolonged unconsciousness

convulsion — violent shaking of the body; a fit

diuretic — medication that causes a person to produce more urine

electrolyte — chemical compound that conducts electricity and controls the balance of fluids in the body

elite — very best at doing something

ether — chemical liquid with fumes that can dull the senses and cause unconsciousness

gene doping — using genetic material (genes) to affect a person's physical makeup

hallucinogenic drug — drug that causes hallucinations (imaginary visions and and feelings)

hormone — natural chemical substance in the body that regulates the activity of body systems

marathon — long-distance running race of 26 miles, 385 yards (42.2 kilometers)

narcotic	drug that dulls the senses and lessens pain
nutritional supplement	substance taken to make up for a particular lack in the diet
opposition	people in a debate who speak against the proposition
phlebotomist	specialist who takes blood samples for laboratory tests
prescription drug	medicine that needs a doctor's prescription before it can be given out or sold
proposition	statement that expresses an opinion or a judgment
refutation	reply to an argument, often based on disagreement over the facts or reasoning
stimulant	drug that causes an increase in activity in part of the body
stroke	sudden blood blockage in the brain
testosterone	natural male hormone that stimulates the male sex characteristics and anabolic activity

Index